THE RADIO WAS GOSPEL

salmonpoetry

Published in 2013 by
Salmon Poetry
Cliffs of Moher, County Clare, Ireland
Website: www.salmonpoetry.com
Email: info@salmonpoetry.com

Copyright © Elaine Feeney, 2013

ISBN 978-1-908836-38-0

COVER DESIGN: *Ray Glasheen*
TYPESETTING: *Siobhán Hutson*
Printed in Ireland by Sprint Print

Salmon Poetry gratefully acknowledges the support of The Arts Council

For the very beautiful, mad, strong women I share my life with. You have been there in your honest parts. Your contribution to my happiness, life, creativity and my vision is perpetual.

Especially for my mother, Catherine,
and my Grandmothers,
Bernadette Cunningham
and
Delia Feeney (RIP)

I am forever in your debt.

Acknowledgments

Acknowledgments are due to the following publications, in which some of these poems first appeared: *The Stinging Fly*, *Cinderella Backwards*, *The Poetry Bus*, *Ex-Border Almanac*, *Irish Left Review*, and *New Planet Cabaret Anthology* (New Island in association with RTÉ, 2013).

"The Radio was Gospel" was recorded and aired on RTÉ Radio 1. "Mass" was recorded for RTÉ Television's *The Gathering* and for Culture Night 2013 on RTÉ Radio 1. Some poems were recorded for Aberdeen Radio's, 'The Literature Show'. "Mass" and a selection of poems were featured on Galway University Radio's series, 'The Portrait of the Artist'.

"The Radio was Gospel" and "Bog Fairies" are works commissioned by artist Petra Berntsson for her exhibition and publication, 'Once Upon Reflection'.

Thank you to Dani Gill and the Cúirt Literature Festival, The Galway Arts Centre, Sarah Clancy, Kit Fryatt and all the Aberdeen gang, Aoibheann McCann, Dave Lordan, Goran, Gasper, Mia and the Slovenian crew, Steve Murray, Celeste Augé, Fionnuala Flanagan, Vinnie Browne and Galway Bay FM, Nuala O' Neill, Séan Rocks, Penny, Evelyn and Sian and all at RTÉ's Arena Show, Joanne Fallon, James Falconer, The Charlie Byrnes gang, all at Dick Mack's in Dingle, Kevin and Susan, Aaron Copeland and all from the UPSTART project, Dimitra Xidous, Liam Quinn, Stephen James Smith and the First Fortnight Sessions, Des and all at Kennys Bookshop, Lorraine Fitzpatrick, James Falconer, Ellen Cranitch and Lyric FM, Kernan Andrews and the *Galway Advertiser*.

Especially to the Salmon troop, big love to Jessie Lendennie and Siobhán Hutson.

Ray Glasheen for the book cover and everything unsaid in-between. Jack for the photography and all the tea, and Finn for perspective, nothing matters unless a superhero is down.

Contents

Salvage

"I'm like that. Either I forget right away or I never forget."

SAMUEL BECKETT, *Waiting for Godot*

Limbo

The weight of the world
is love
under the burden
of solitude
under the burden
of dissatisfaction
the weight,
the weight we carry
is love

ALLEN GINSBERG

Sniff

The rose tree in our garden
flowers in a rush
to satisfy my mother.

Butter yellow petals
smother the tarmac,

don't they smell lovely?

she says,
holding the yellow rose
fist-tight between
her rubber-gloved fingers.

She dead-heads fallen ones,
those rusty and stink.

Lovely, I shout back
through the years of
wallowing wind.

All I smell is steaming hot rain,
placing down gambles
with the tarmac muck.

Horse Dealers

Horse dealers
came into our drive
like ventriloquist dolls.

With their thick-thighs,
puffed out jackets,
pipes in yellowed fingers,
hollowed out shoulders.

Pieces of cracked wavin
in fists gripped tight
to unsettle the earth,
or crack a mare's rump,
or weather a son
unused to dealing code.

Horsemen came into my world
with the importance
of amphitheatre,
the cold charisma of wilting tulips
on an Easter altar,

with all the mummering
of wild grass blades
nudging to summer,

their pockets
deep with the promises
of Moses.

But they weren't to be trusted.

Horsemen
Dealers

With their swaggering big fingers.

With their eyes wild to the wind,
with their foot shuffling language,
their unsettled eyes darting.

Their coarse fearless souls
as they spat words to the dry earth,

every beast was the same,
once it obeyed.

For the Nuns, For the Nuns

In Memory of Thomas Cunningham

You look like a boxer,
an old crooner from the eighties, like
Ray Reardon with oily jet-black tresses
flattened by Vaseline hair tonic.

You wear a suit and blue collar yet
you speak wildly of the pope,
the Vatican Council, Bishop Casey.

The Cathedral, the Auggi,
the Claddagh Church, the Mervue flats,

the state of the place –
the bus-pass, the bed-nap-pass.

You hail De Valera's constitution,
fantastic parchment inscribed
with the right wing of God.

You speak of heretics, the Lantern bar.

How you fear the taxman,
how you're going to set the tax terriers
loose on my dad's heels.

You bike ride to Lydon's
bakery for years,
you bake bleached breads
for those in Barry Avenue.

I'm seven, stuffed down, awkward.
My face like a waxy bread pan cover.

I'm collecting bread pan covers for the nuns,
for the black babies, Grandad.

For the nuns, for the nuns, for the nuns.

For a presentation for the Presentation nuns.

Well Miss Elaine,
dance a hopscotch then for Dev!
Then I'll tell you a story about Johnny McGorey –
Will I begin it a grá? That's all that's in it!

Eagerness thumped dead.

I'm wrapping myself in the world
of the bread pan papers,
to save the black babies.

You tell me another story –
spark up a cigarette;

Jack, Jack, my shirt is black, what'll I do for Sunday?
Go to bed and cover your head and don't come out until Monday –

Sloppy butts mash between long yellow
talons of fingers that iced my birthday cakes.

Iced like the theatre in Harrogate
where I watched the Scottish play.

Did I collect enough wrappers from
Lydons for you Loveen?

You reach to your saggy shiny suit pocket,
you pull a coin –
a silver shiny one –

the sharp bird beaked one,
the heavy fifty pee one.

Buy an icecream loveen.

Me with all the wrappers of bread pans
for the Presentation nuns.

What'll they do with all the waxy paper?
Sure they can't eat the paper
abroad in Africa, tis swelling up their bellies.

And what about all the stamps?
Stamp bread pan paper mountains
is it them nuns are building beyont in Africa?

For the nuns, for the nuns.

I give the fifty pee to the black babies,
hundreds of bread pan papers for the black babies.

For the nuns, for the nuns, for the nuns.
For their mountain.

Trapping Badgers

When my brother wanted to trap badgers,
off we set, three Phileas Foggers.

Iceberg lettuce leaves, rose petals, ropes,
digestive biscuits and a hand signal in case anyone was

taken down the snare trap to their death.
He was the oldest so we believed

him when he said he had watched
them running in the field

deep in the night. We believed him when
he said that they could smell girls

and they'd call them to the trap, we believed
him when he said the sett ran wild with rabbits.

We flithered in mist and the rain,
deep in the heart of badger country,

then sat for hours waving lettuce leaves
silently at the sett keystone. Turn of May and

it was to something new. Dipping sheep,
cutting their coarse stink wool from their hollow backs,

dagging greasy maggots –
besides we had given up on seeing a badger.

We had spotted them through him. He'd tell us
and we loved his stories. I listened for years.

Setting traps, trapping badgers.
Now we've hardly a hand to wave

from one hole to another, the death
signal for help's long forgotten,

and we've taken to our setts
as if we never hunted.

Junior Infants

Scoil Croí Naofa, Athenry

I screamed at my new teacher
and then at the Virgin Mary.

Jars of coloured blocks,
deep pits of sand and water –

children with big bags
like bees unstuck from their honey-hives.

I was mad as hell's fire she left me there
at four years and some days,

with a bag and a brown beaker of leaky milk,

with navy blue slippers, different to the sanctioned
coarse black ones,

pretty, like her, with an
orange puppet up the shinsock.

She let my hand go slightly, yet
her fear was to the tip of her slim ringfinger.

I learned very little
inside those unplastered walls

with those girls and the sour milk and
the big–black–banana–skinned bins,

except that the drummer has the best
job in the band, nuns wear their anger

around their crackled lips like cailleachs
and separating is intensely practical.

The Radio was Gospel

for Andrea

I had a Granny who used to tell me
with large fat sweaty hugs,
that I was her favourite,
she loved the long limbs of me.

But all of us were and none of us were
and children can smell that love and lies.

These are dangerous lessons.

Our mother's lessons took
longer to learn.

Early in September
she walked us home,
small children by the hand,
miles and miles and miles
taking a long road to Mountain North,
with its marshes and branches,
we thought she had gone mad.

I rushed and picked blackberries
before they would rust and shoved them
deep to the dark cave
of my tupperware beaker.

Her radio was gospel, the
mechanical throat in our kitchen.

The farming weather,
the sea forecast, the promise,

knots and winds and waves

from Carnsore to Oranmore,
from Mizen and Malin.

Gay and Nell and all the
Mondays at Gaj's women
sat at our kitchen table
and saved mothers
from multiple labours.

And while they'd still cook the dinner,
they'd educate their daughters.

And when I was pregnant
and asked about labour,
she weeded out my flowerbeds,
washed my windows,
changed the beds,
for that stretching could snap the red
cord around a small neck.

When I married she gave
me jam-jar advice on sex.

Nothing is easy, as I am a mother
balancing on a fulcrum

of rage and love,
loss and end.

A brittlehoneycombed foundation.

When I would die from brainclotfear,

she swore if I stroked,
she'd help me to sleep
deep in Switzerland,
dressed in decent clothes.

My daughter is sick,

she would say

but she will be ok,

she would say.

And all the weeds choking the roses,
the endless sheets of polythene plastic,
covered over by fresh chipped
bark in our front garden.

Now I sit on her bed
and trace my finger over her books
and clothes and bits of ends,
glass-jars, tissues,
costume jewellery,
photos of her grandkids.

She'd love good rings, she tells me.

But she has virtue
in powerful proportion,

and diamond rings
and emerald things

come at some cost.

We salted the guts from the fruits,
then made blackberry tarts.

Busy insects ran wild in the red water.

These days together,
are her chattels,
they are her rings
and diamond things.

This is our love.

Middle Ireland

He is a hard backed Oxford Concise Dictionary
with reinforced glass spine.

She is Cecilia Holman-Lee in a tooth fairy
costume in a sharp Brown Thomas window.

He is a cotton woven Kartel polo-shirt, dipped in
baby blue, spruced with a classy cologne.

She is the last ever produced
Black-Knight-Denby butter dish lid.

He is Nano Nagle's wet dream.
She is Olivia Newton John stepping out

on Saturday Night Fever
with plimsoles and curtain song-sarong.

They are Saddam Hussein's Shiraz Saturday
guests,
sipping from chipped Waterford crystal.

Crayon Rubbings

They stood bolt upright,
like waxy soldiers at invisible gates
of Tiananmen Square.

They had flown from China
in a panda-eating-bamboo box.

It was the first time I had ever seen a panda.

Soon they'd be for viewing
in Dublin Zoo.

In landscape on buttery yellow paper,
I brought a spidery line for a walk.

I coloured bulging
Chinese balloons
moments before bursting –

red, green, yellow, blue.

Then I killed it.

I dug a black crayon deep
all over the page.

Calmer now for the etching.

With the back of a steel spoon
I scraped out a brother,
smoke from a chimney,
I etched out a sun,
a mother in an apron
a tired labrador,

a red rose-bush
some rainbow fields and a blue see-saw,
a silver gate,

a baby in a brown pram,
a father holding lead reins
of a nervous roan mare.

I scraped and scraped and scraped.

The crayon rubbings
slept in under my short nails that night
and the rainbow sun at the front of the house?

I could swear it glowed in the dark.

Bog Fairies

for Matt

The heather like pork belly cracked
underneath my feet –

The horizon like nougat,
melted its pastel line at the heat edge
blue fading to white light.

We stacked rows of little
houses for bog fairies –

wet mulchy sods
evaporating under our small palms.

Crucifixions of dry brittle crosses
formed the skeleton –
my narrow ankles parallel to them.

Coarse and tough like the marrow of the soul,
like the skeltons crucified under the peat.

The turf will come good,

my father said

when the wind blows to dry it.

We dragged ten-ten-twenty bags
with the sulphury waft of cat piss,
along a track dotted
with deep black bogholes,
over a silver door,
like a snail's oily trail
leaving a map for the moon,
for bog fairies to dance on the mushy earth.

And behind the door once upon sometime
old women sat in black shawls
bedding down irregulars
and putting kettles on to boil
for fresh labouring girls.

But I was gone.

I was dragging Comrades from the Somme
I was pulling Concords in line with Swedish giants
I was skating on the lake in Central Park
I was crouched in the green at Sam's Cross
I was touring Rubber-Soul at Hollywood Bowl
I was marching on Washington with John Lewis

I was in the Chelsea Hotel with Robert Mapplethorpe,
he was squatting on my lap with his lens,
swearing to God to Janis Joplin I could find her a shift,
nothing is impossible when you blow like that girlfriend.

I sang Come As You Are in Aberdeen with union converse,
petrol blue eye liner and mouse holes in my Connemara jumper.

I was anyone but me.
I was anywhere but here.

We rushed to hurry before the summer light would fade
because animals needed to be washed and fed –

And turf needed to be stacked –

And all the code talk of our youth
would be said behind our hands.

Because light was the ruler as it closed in around us,
like the dark on the workmen
deep in the Channel Tunnel that night.

The black light killed the purple heather —

Yet I danced on the crackle in the dusk —

I crackled on the dust in the heather —

My dance on the heather turned to dust.

Goats and Lambs

On a beach they passed
over goats and coins
for her.

A dark orange veil
ran wild in the wind,
its anchor; a willowy stick
of girl shadow.

There are nuclear rumours somewhere
or another tonight;

Iraq Russia Turloughmore Clarinbridge

I pull my orange quilt cover over
my head and listen to
new lambs outside crying for their mothers.

I pray for the girleen
I pray for nuclear disarming
I pray for the lambing

Chocolate

In memory of Delia Feeney

1.

Sr. Alphonsus slapped me
across the thigh with
my own dimpled tin whistle –

a pencil pursed between
her pale cracked lips
and the snap cracked
under the shy part of my gymslip –

girls must
wear socks
not tights
socks socks

2.

At break-time in the yard
pretty girls teach me shyness
and rank and fileness.

They throw my
gymslip shoes over
King John's wall
into the supermarket car-park.

I run there and
meet my Grandmother
shopping simply;
buttermilk, bacon,
a turnip,
wheatmeal,
eggs, stamps and a Dairy Milk
chocolate bar.

She gives me the chocolate bar
and teaches me love.

I am torn between
being late and
melting chocolate.

     3.

Her green ruler
like a banana leaf,
solidified in Ghana,
teaches me punctuality
over warm
chocolate squares —

child dear child
dear child dear

She has taught me shame.

And I the dear child
and scholar
learn to flourish
with great hate.

First Shift

I was lifting legs bound
in striped woollen tights
heavy Doc Martens, that gave me cow legs.

Heather Shimmer lippy
painted on my pus
my eyes as gritty rusty
shutters in the riots –
gassed up to their iris
in the Temperance Hall,
slow dancing in a circle
to Four Non Blondes,
telling us to wake up.

D'ya want ta dance with my friend?
Would ya shift him?

As ferocious scrawny kittens just born
stroking tongues longing for their mother's teat –

stretching up and down the side of a
canvas bag in a murky barrel of rain water –

hardly breathing, suffocating at the
delicate nape of a neck –
crawling to air and light.

D'ya want ta dance with my friend?

Eventually breath
is a gift given back
and air is the only thanks.

Was it your first shift?

between botched drags of
a nippered fag.

Yeah, but I've drowned before
and I've been birthed,
but I can't remember much of it.

Did ya dance with my friend?
Would ya dance with me?

D'ya know maybe ya'd shift the pair of us?

Monopoly Player

He defends the final solution.

A socialist orator for social occasions.

A man for all seasons.

Ailesbury Road and Crumlin
bought in clean sweep.

He bows to the Baroness,
because she's a great speaker

And can lick the back
of a miner's greasy newspaper
for a wink and a nod.

A bad word to say for everyone.

A sword on Monday
and a shield by Friday.

He paints on deep red
Chelsea smiles,
heads to town.

Joker to the lads,
then takes refuge
in Batman's cave.

A mover and shaker –
A great man for a deal –
For the spit and shake –

A great man to everyman
yet no man at all.

Dead Dog

for Claire Haynes

I dyed my hair marmalade orange
the same day the dog died
in a half-barrel of rain water.

I cupped my hair into a speel
on top of my head,

forcing out mousy blonde –

held tight under the water –

struggling.

Balancing against
the olive enamel sink
in my best friend's bathroom.

There was a dog dead in
the fore-ground
of the land,

a scattering of puppies whined.

It used to be Guernica.

Now it's barely a dead hotel's watercolour,

the rewashes didn't tone out the rust.

The dog was dead.

I was off dying my hair and
galavanting with my
skithery best friend.

But what could I have saved?

What could I have saved at thirteen and a half?

Everything was semi-permanent,

even the rust.

Daughter

I am a farmer's daughter.

Bad sessht to them
twas a terrible ordeal
sure twas terrible
jusht terrible
arra shtop, shtop entirely,
poor fuckereeens.

The sibilant consonant
speel secures the passport –

I spend years shredding.

Overalls

Odoury oiled overalls
overpowers evening telly.

Nervous eyeballing,
chipboard flakes fly
as a hollow chair is
dragged to the jomb
of a pine door.

A hairy descendant of a tribe
who comments airily
on basts in meadows,
knuckled head rock breakers.

Pricks of men with
fists big as rotted hearts.

His eyes bloodstained
like the licorice pipes they suck on,
that weep from welding sparks.

To fill bellies.
To put food on a table.
To the weatherman on telly.

In Connemara seeped deep in marsh,
avoiding the clicking tock-in.

Searching for decent poitín,
to numb Sunday's
middle class make-believe.

Barren women in wool
strong jumpers of steely shades.

Easter Eggs

The boy got a Yorkie egg
with big black wheels,

a cardboard box shaped like
an old American truck,

a bag of chunky chocolates
lined its belly.

The girl got a Cadbury's egg
with lots of thick chocolate.

Time dashed with little respect
only to serve the ever setting sun.

Mornings stolen when their young breath would
mix with chatter out under the front porch –

when craft and play
were the only currency –

and home made paper watches
were stuck to narrow wrists with sellotape.

When time on the clock face stood
still until it rained away.

They are gone to other people,
to make giants out of them.

Charles Bukowski is my Dad

He stands with me in the
best-dressed-lady-line,
holding my pearl lace
umbrella open to the
ravaging Galway rain.

He calls me up on
blue Mondays and gives me
whiskey on bold Fridays.

He fills up my father-space
He fills up my mind-space
He fills up my hot-water bottle

His advice fills up my cheer
and revives my rotted liver,

but that's a small price to pay

because Bukowski's my Dad.

He's my feather pillow
and my guitar string.

He's my soccer coach and sex therapist.

He paints my nails pepperminty green
and sings raindrops keep falling on my head
on wicked trips to the racetrack.

But that's a small price to pay
because Bukowski's my dad.

Ambush

Yerra, they'll never shoot me in my own county.

Michael Collins

Mass

Mass will be said for no more bad language and gambling and wanking that the Athenry boys are doing, down the back of the castle, down the back of the couch, all the punching and hitting and groaning, moaning at the Turlough boys, the Clarinbridge boys, the boys from Killimordaly, down the back of the Presentation grounds.

There will be mass when you lose at the Galway Races and for the saving of your soul if you take the boat to Cheltenham.

There will be a mass for when the horse runs, and when the horse dies, and for the bookies who win and the punters who win,

and the bookies who lose and the punters who lose.

There will be mass for hare coursing and flask-filling.

There will be mass for your Inter Cert and your twenty-first, There will be a filling-out-your-CAO-form mass.

Mass will be held in the morning before the exams, mass will be held in the evening for your bath.

There'll be a special mass on Saturday afternoon for your Granny. There will be a mass for your Granny's boils and aches and black lungs and ulcers and spots and diabetes and psychosis.

There'll be a mass for the anointing of the bollix of the bull above in the field near the closh over the railway bridge.

Mass will be held before the College's Junior B Hurling Final, it will be held for the Connaught Cup Junior A Regional Final in wizardry and sarcasm.

Mass will be held on top of the reek for the arrogant and meek, and the bishop will arrive by eurocopter. There will be a mass to get him up in one piece and back in one piece. Mass will be held in the outhouse.

Mass will be held for the safe arrival of new lambs and the birthing of ass foals.

Mass will be held in your uncle's sitting room but his neighbours will be envious and later stage a finer mass.

There will be a mass to find you a husband, and a few masses to pray he stays.

There will be a good intentions mass. Your intentions if they're good will come true. Mass will be held for your weddings and wakes and when you wake up.

Mass will be held for the Muslim conversion.

Mass will be held for George Bush.

Mass will be held for the war on terror.

Mass will be held for black babies and yellow babies and the yellowy black babies.

Mass will not be held for red babies. They have upset Pope John-Paul.

Mass will be held for your brother when he gets the meningitis from picking his nose. Mass will be held for your cousins when they stop going to mass.

Mass will be held for the harvest and the sun and the moon and a frost and a snow and for a healthy spring and red autumn, for a good wind and no wind, and for a good shower and a dry spell, and for the silage and the hay and the grass and the turf.

There will be a saving-of-the-turf day. There will be a saving-of-the-hay day. There will be a saving-my-soul day.

There will be a mass for the fishing fishermen.

There will be multiple masses for Mary around August when she did all the appearing.

There will be a good mass when the statue cries rusty tears. There will be a good mass and a great collection.

Mass will be held for the cloud people.

Mass will be held for apparitions and anniversaries and weddings and baptisms.

Mass will be held to church your sinned body after giving birth, there will be mass to wash your unclean feet.

Mass will be held for all your decisions so you don't have to blame yourself.

There will be mass for the poor dead Clares.

There will be mass for the Black Protestants if Paisley allows it. Mass will be held for the De Valeras and the Croke Park goers.

There will be a mass for the conversion of the Jews (and their collection).

There will be a mass for the communion class, there will be a mass for the no-name club non-drinkers. There will be a giving-up-smoking-the-Christian-way mass.

There will be a mass for the Christian Angels, only Christian ones.

There will be no mass for your freedom, but the air will be pea sweet and the sky will clear.

Mass will not be held for the souls of your gay sons.

Mass will not be held for song-and-dance makers, the apple cart topplers.

There will be no women's mass.

There will be no mass solely by women for women. Your daughters will not hold mass.

There are very strict rules for the masses.

The Stinking Rose

1.

The earth is crumbling her ties and shirts and lace and silk and
leather and cufflink and mouth and limb and heart and liver
and spit and muscle and gunk and tendon and fat and nails and
hair and glump and sinew and gut and throat –

She's burning down the Taj Mahal

To the industrial Ferry Buildings
to the Embarcadero's dead mute floors

Through the flaming punk haired hippies
down Haight-Ashbury

Through the scalding damp
of scorched mouths from
Eyre Square to Times Square –

to a queued up orgasm in North Korea

silent cries over in Brisbane

to the freezing in Moscow

cry- for the Egyptian dead this morning

cry- for the Syrian dead this morning

cry- for the dead all dead mornings.

2.

In October's fog
the Venice street vendors
make masquerade masks
for Festival February –

before their stinking city sinks –

they lick and love and ponce and pose –

all mouthless and comeless and laughless

through the visible fumbling fist of Wall Street –
through the halls of Treasury Whore Houses –

the krankelling roads and wheels
that rolled from Rome and Greece.

We made a road

they cried

and look where we walked.

3.

Girls' hearts oozing squeezing the boys fixing their poise who
are painting the ends of their flesh and panting and petting and
stuffing their pores and tattooing their feet who are occupying
and denying to this uncatchable war an unfathomable feeling
we shove swollen fists to our burnished mouths and choke cries
and laughs wet-tents beautiful-beards smells-drift rainbow-flags
and dogs are called different commands.

4.

She is sitting down and crying with cutworms at her feet
She is sitting down and crying with cutworms at her feet

In the hole at Alcatraz they waved their hands in front of their
faces and saw light.

Even in the pitch black dark, they saw some light –

and threw cent coins in the air day after day just to find them.

She plays the game over and over –

and then screams from her scalds –
and her poisoned pithy veins –

coin after coin after coin after coin –

smoking her anger to the ocean she is churning buying
dropping believing and dying and selling and breathing and
ending and going and moving and coming and crackling and
spitting and firing and splintering and gassing and laughing –

and she screams in the hole

I have sold my soul to panhandlers on Union Square
I have sold my soul for the roads of Rome
I have sold my soul for the fools who fuck me
I have sold my sold for rough diamonds and love
I have sold my soul for angry Gods abundance
I have sold my soul for oil and liver
I have sold my soul for spice and silk
I have sold my soul for church and gem
I have sold my soul for what I can't eat

You bought me for Snake Oil and Beads
You bought me for Snake Oil and Beads

And sold me for dollars and six shooter pistols

I am a Stinking Rose
I am a Stinking Rose
I am a Stinking Rose

Electric Picnic

for Stephen Murray

Apsu of the abyss near Athlone
feels her little breasts thumping –
Her heart kept shy to the world
by two delicate strings
and a layer of neon.

She has flowers in her hair –
plastic cerise coarse things
knotted in little wispy strands.

Tiamat the void
sticks her welly in the ground –
stands still.

A flat-bellied Pompeii girl
with a whirl and then frozen –
she fires her head to the ground
a swan dive to limbo –
moving impy hips to the
disorderly drums.

Ansher and Kishar from Kerry
like pasty Italian tourists
examine the ash to stay safe.

They came to hear riffs and chords
And watch capos and placement
And rub girls
And runaway

And the mouse on the stage is gnawing
And the altar is the place of worship
And the boys dance raw-headed
And run fingers through divilry

The girls like peccadillo's flurry –
stick their red wellies to the earth

They have been to Pompeii with their parents
They have perfected this move
They have practiced
These are good girls

They have danced in the back garden in the spring-time,
in only their pyjamas and glow sticks

Void and Abyss and the
hiss of the sounds
and the banging clatter,
fold their skin to each other as
towels fresh from their mother

cocooned and dry –

driven half mad by the moon
driven half mad by time escaping.

When the muck

settled and the dawn visited

Ansher and Kishar awaken

get breakfast

falafels, veggie burgers.

Shots of wheatgrass
Shots of fuck grass and olives
Shots of vulgar and vulva and hummus –

body and soul

mind and God
to soak the spirit
to line the mind.

They fear the flood
and stock up for her –

For she will come
among the heavens of
canvas and smoke
and crystal and laughs –

For she will come among steam
and rain and fog and pig

At dawn the Pompeii girls
take to the bubbles

and the bath is a soak in prosecco
and the grit is their sugar scrub
in the Body and Soul half mad with fixation
half mad with fame-coloured-flaneurs.

All watering eyes
all blind
all cavorting
all cleansing
all hooring
all laughing
all screaming
and lying
to prying
And fluttering –

trying, tasting, fearful in the festival thirst.

Russia

Russia, I can't find you.

I've traced the crumbs from
the Winter Palace,
I have killed the Tsars
and painted
blood on the walls.

The oil has frozen in Moscow
just for pleasure.

Your victorious Stalingrad.
Your brave men.

I long for bread queues,
but I'm on my way to France.

Soldiers on the news
marching in mad lines,
kicking their legs hip-high
like demented can-can dancers.

A century on, the sluttish cobble stones of the
Victorian dead salute you

blood on the floor,
your women in Dublin's
boutique hoor hotels with
iPhones and Finlandia vodka,

with men who'd rip their
kidneys out for a hard fuck.

When the plane lands in
Charles de Gaulle,

we wade like divil's
through France's lushness,
through Vichy unspoilt.

But I'm searching for Russia.

For men with woeful sad faces

nearer the men I know than the
French teenager I
buy peach apricots from.

They'd never scorch their earth –
or take you in their long man arms and

shake you –

make you dance for them.

Russia I'm here on Mont Blanc
camping with boys beautiful like
ice sculpted Swatch watches –

I miss waking up beside you
I want frozen vodka shots
I want your broken teeth
I want your faded rose thorn tattoos

I don't want French boys
without a trace of beard.

Russia I would open borders for you,
I would open borders for you,
if I could only get near.

Biteens

for Sarah Clancy

Little biteens of people, pieces all over the raven pavements and sprayed on the cracked gutters, bits of them strewn on the carpeted lanes, and propped against wheelie bins like the carcasses of bored butlers, bits of them.

Biteens of people, shards of anoraks and faded canvas shopping bags, sloven splinters of their teeth, angles of jawlines where jaws used to sit, pieces of people, god help them, dead to rush hour, dead.

Silver wisps of greased dandruffy-dead-hair.

Dead waiting at the bus stop dead waiting at the counter top dead waiting at the social shop dead waiting at the hospital drop dead waiting at the morgue spot.

Putting biteens of sharred shoulders to the wind, their half bodies and eaten bones.

The blush-blown look of the cretins, blown out of our way down alleys in corpo houses on free bus spins on acid on nebulisers on tea on glue and sugar on lithium on valium on sadnesss and sorrow on beauty on faith.

Biteens of people, pieces of them, imagine it.

Light a candle or two.

For their mass cards and petitions, for their shopping bags for our lady and their prescriptions, for their mothers for their missing sons and for their saints.

If the Wind Blows South

for Jude and Eoin

If the wind blows south,
your eyes will fix like that forever.

The newsreader on Monday called it spectacular.

Men clambered on top of cars
spectacularly looking for their children.

Like a spectacular scene
from a Superman movie.

In last night's dream,
from under muddy waters,
I saved a boy with a hurl
and scooped him to my chest
and ran the unfamiliar Japanese
territory looking for somewhere
spectacular to put him.

On Thursday I stood at Christchurch,
watched children wave flags
with green shamrock melting on their waxed skin,

looked at men on the ground on the ha'penny bridge,

saw a dog lick his owner's wound in Heuston,

marching bands whirled and giddied,

a man sang Christy in the Arlington.

I looked to their hands,

to the spitting French tourists –
to the redbrickedbracked on Dublin castle –
to the jeering and cheering and waving –

to the thousands of eyes fixed forever –

to the melting skin,
as children
arise and fall in the Dublin crowds
arise and fall in the Japanese waters.

Then I looked to the sky
and looked for God.

Begging Letters, 1913

1.

A liberties woman
sent begging letters
from her tenement table.

Each Thursday she licked
the gluey envelope
with a sharp hairy tongue.

2.

I am a very good Roman Catholic your Grace,
my childers, in order to avoid the scourge of
the nakedness, need your generous kind spirit.
Would ya spare a couple of shillings
for the food and for the shoes?

Otherwise I'll be left
with no alternative but to
protest them in the most awful of
protestations down to the doors of the
Protestant Church –

Which isn't nearly as lovely
as your own palace.

And what's worse –

I'd really hate to have to do it.

Isolate

'Oh God I hate being out of the city
because I know who's out here' –
THE COLOUR OF FEAR

First I stopped talking to the ducks,
they kept their heads down.

I couldn't read their expression,
beakless pusses on them.

Then the foxes started to get in on me –
they'd chat but once I'd freed them

from their snare, they'd fuck off into the night –
kept me up all night one night in the freezing fog.

Thanked me with a sexy soiree around their den, let me
in on all the secrets of others. They knew lots of secrets being

so clever, (and sly) sometimes they told me the sheep put their head down deep in the water troughs and the kids do it too, just like commoners.

I think the sheep are alright, I said, woolly and stumbly, but ok.
We tried to keep the party going, but there was a stink in the air.

Later I saw one half eaten, blood dripping down the foxes sharp jaw and short neck. It was dark, but I could swear the fox winked at me.

The half lamb wasn't up to much.
Then I decided I'd ignore the traffic.

It was always coming at me in such a hurry and so scattered.
Eventually I gave up on the whole lot of them –

I just did, the nights were howling and long
but the days had less fear, were clearer

and I was less inclined to upset anything,
only myself if I knocked over my tea or let the fire go dead.

Sylvia Plath You Are Dead

Sylvia Plath you are dead.
Your tanned legs are dead.

Your smile is dead, and
Massachusetts will mourn her

girl on lemonade days,
on sunshine days.

She will mourn her on dark days
when screaming girls go mad

in maternity wars
and scream in domestic wards,

and cry handfuls of slathery salty water
in kitchens over blue ironing boards.

Sylvia Plath you are dead,
and girls try rubbing out stretched marks

off olive silver skin, till they bleed.
Tiny baby cocoons cry in the hallways

till candy-framed windows fog over,
their minds, their aprons, their skirts,

their college ways, where there were no lessons on

tears. Silvery Plath the moon howls at us
taunted by strong winds, staying the course,

out the garden paths, strong gusts blow heads
off ivy's shoulder, but heather keeps a low profile

her bright purple head down.

Therapy

Today I started therapy.

I sat on an Ikea chair.

I want Dean Martin to be my Dad
I want the freakish gross look
I want to like breastfeeding
I want my sons to be dentists
I want liposuction for my belly

Ask them not to be angry
just in your head
or write a nice letter
then burn it.

The fantasies aren't safe.

Least of all that one where you ride the winged horse
through the closed window of the Bishop's Palace.

But it's a metaphorical smash up.

Surely he stays safe.

The horse isn't shod in any case.

Live a little Miss Therapy.

I threaten her and tell her
I am nothing without my fantasies.

I win.

She gives me other numbers.

Some scripts of coloured pills to be filled
before I get to the cliff edge,

she thinks winning is what makes me proud.

Saving Turf with Leopold Bloom

One raised eyebrow, the other in
place down the back of Davy Byrne's.

Sure twas as well you Molly honey
as any other bit of skirt

a wide hand gripped
to the curve
of her moon arse.

And the state of things.

Have you seen the state of the
fucking place?

Your working class denim
Your working man's flaneur flair
has failed to give off anything
only North Tipperary and East Galway.

You have come to find Joyce,

the Trieste sea calls
the hooring women call,

yet your mind is full
of Nenagh and Fermoy
of Abbey and Athenry
and New Ross.

Its not what the locals feel
Leopold, Leopold,
it's not what the locals think.

They don't think, Leo.
They mumble and eat and shit.
Then fumble to their deaths like ark rats,

to share shallow graves with thieves and
with charred bones of tobacco spitters
and paddy cap wearers.

Leopold Bloom it's what's inside yourself man.

You weren't born for a sleán.

Don't get dragged back into that one.

Leopold, Leopold, Leopold Bloom.

Just stay here,
just stay away.

Salvage

*"Praise the God of all, drink the wine
and let the world be the world."*

FRENCH PEASANTS

Sting

I globe a piece of
red playdough out on
my small wet palm.

I flatten it with my thumb,
melt it
bit by bit
leaf by leaf,

slobby and imperfect.

The caper green
wrapped around
cut chicken wire.

With a Japanese knife-sharpener
I carve the tip of a cocktail
stick thorn.

The thorns claw deep
through my wet skin.

I do not bleed.

Little Picasso

for Ray

And did I feel breaking light on my face
in the early hours,
walking the road home drunk from town,
over Divilly's hill and past Kilkelly's boreen,
tearing out ditches with my mad grin and
hearing kids screaming,
loose from the pubs in my wake –
premature like china peapods bursting?

And did I hear my father whistling from
the shower on Saturday evenings,
a threadbare towel wrapped roughly round
his narrow freckled waist –
lashings of frothy foam a puckish mask on his face,
sharply sliced bare in solid strokes
to jubilant red raw spit nicks –
small fresh little diamonds,
dotted with white tissue corners?

And did I smell petrol spice each time
I poured it from the red can,
to the heat swollen belly of the mower,
years after years to walk it
over the same low lying mossy field?

And did I feel your
wide handsome face in that narrow space
where my shoulder blade, long lost to my skin folds
and breast curve meet?

Did I feel your warm breath on my narrow
hairs upright,
did I whisper that love can only be found at the end

of the story for then
neither fool can cheat the ending with
poor instinct?

Then it's over and only the walls can hold our truth.

Did I taste the salt of your tears at break-times in the grounds
of the Athenry Pres,
long before you were my lover, those creeping long days
in St. Peter's, when you talked to the basketball rings?

When we brought imaginary stiff friends home on Friday
evenings for tea?

On those wet dusky Wexford evenings when real friends
should have been round.

Did I hear your young requests declined that bold paintings
could sit at the table and eat?

Did I hear angry whispers that imaginary friends have no place
among silent crystal?

That the table was no place for imaginings, the table was no
place for colour.

There are stories to be told and retold and learned by heart
like useless division tables, those awkward little arrowheads
dividing up chambers to ordered strings,

like pale stuffed artichoke hearts, blocking each from the other.

When the silence ended, did the silence begin?

There was no place at the table for drawings,

only silver cutlery from Sheffield,

only white linen cloth,
only strain and salt.

Or did I imagine it all, in the space where light drops and the
moon turns her face down, did I somehow dream of the place
our life was, and unearth a place where those dreams should
have been left to sleep?

And maybe in the end, they were right to sanction their tables,
maybe in the end they were right to set their borders.

For what ever came from our wild imaginings lover?

And did our paintings ever make polite conversation?

Child

I love the very

hard bones

of you

every piece

I made from scratch,

every dimpled

waxy patch of your skin.

Your heart chambers

Your lungs

and soft toenails

each bone

solid

knitting together.

I love the

very hard bones of you

your long limbs

made by scratch

in me.

I Told You So

I knew you were going to die.
I knew I would see your face,
an early obituary –

Your grin and freckle and
wobbly insecure muscle.

It was as if it was always going to be,

If I could pick the boys I knew would die
and hold them in a tight mad midnight embrace,

I would have picked you.

Now you are dead
there's no embrace –

there's no comfort in

I told you so's

Screamed out to the western seaboard
Screamed out to the murky dock waters

There is no use in my knowledge and
no one madder than myself at my anguish
and anger and no embrace soft enough to
hold tight dark demons of young boys,

too young to talk about rage
that feeds on small bodies,
before language has even time to arrive.

Dublin Town

for my mother

I am with you in Dublin
as it rains down on the Quays,
we dance to strange sounds
on Grafton Street then sit in Bewley's
and in the bars round College Green.

I am with you in the clash of the cricket bats,
the unfamiliar sounds as
we pour cheap wine from a paper bag.

We are as Vikings down Woodquay,
our chipped bones bare to the freezing fog.

We are falling over the cobbles,
dancing on Leeson Bridge.

I am with you in Stephen's Green in the sunshine
at the Magdalene statue, frozen from her cold.

I am locked in a duffel coat listening
to the Pet Shop Boys in Clery's,
then tired at the zoo.

I am with you in Christmas tree twinkles,
over the ice rinks,
the breaking waves out at Sandymount,
barely there,
all our plans, and love and freedom together
under the Dart Station at Tara Street drinking pints.

I am alone in the Martello Tower
in nineteen-ninety-nine
whoring myself to Joyce and the apocalypse.

I am with you in red lipstick
I am with you in our blushed cheap silks
I am with you in your knits and in your lost dropped stitches

I am with you in loss

I am with you in Dublin.

Indulgence

There are indulgent things;

carafes of red wine,

soft socks,

lavender baths.

And then you.

Shy like the lip of a mountain

teased by the rushing waterfall,

black silk inked semi-colon'd jaw,

shut tight.

The expectancy of a long list.

I love your punctuation.

My full arms hold me wavering over you.

I have come to watch,

to bring the cold of my

nose tip to your warm face.

There are indulgent things;

honey on warm cinnamon bread,

poached eggs, good paper,

petrol fillers, fantasies.

And then you.

There are no indulgent pillows on this bed.

There is nothing

only you in white sheets for

day-dream-trippers.

There are no children in my head

or chugging my wrists,

clunking up my ear space.

I watch your fingertip

trace a comma

on the rump of my wide hip.

Ray La Montagne plays Shelter.

Our breath, a scene-shifter,

a showman flies in

through the gap in the

white wooden window.

Pity the Mothers

Pity the mothers
who weathered their skin
to raise their sons to die.

Pity their routine,
the daily stretching table
ferociously making ends meet.

Pity the mothers who told their
sons the world was tough and wild –

to have them sold out in the early hours
of mornings' immutable stage,
fresh and stung.

Brave the world!

they should have said –

Brave its bold beauty!

Brave the world my brave sons

and be beautiful!

Fear is a choking kite string.

Fear is a punctuating dictator.

Fear will drive you half insane
and there's no spirit in
half a cup of anything.

Fear will wake your sleep
and damn your
first born nerves.

There is no fertility in fear
no function, no performance.

Be a kite
Be yellow
Be bold
Be mad

Don't step at the edge of it
all and send your body half-way
forward to the sea-froth.

Pity the bags, shoes, boots, hurls
mothers left by the door.

The endless soups and syrups
The forever effort
The long lasting kisses they left on young jaws

To send them to the world fearful
and then feared.

To send them to the world with pity
and then pitied.

Pity the mothers
with their strong
elbows worn from effort.

Struggling against headwinds –
sanding the grain
in the wrong direction.

Pity the mothers
who weathered their skin
just to raise their sons to die.

Ryan Giggs is a Ride

for Jack

1.

I stuck Ryan Giggs pictures
on my blue walls,
down on the skirting boards,
match stickers
all over my wardrobe
and on my window sill.

I stuck Ryan Giggs letters
in the green post-box
on the corner of
Court Lane and High Street,

like a desperate pyrotechnic lover.

I begged him to love me so
I stuck in the language of Shakespeare.

I should have
turned up at his door
and asked him for a ride.

Or married his brother.

I wasted lots of paper.

Then we lost contact.

I started wearing
black crushed velvet
and smoking pot.

I started biting my nails hard
and chasing boys with
back issues of X-Men.

2.

I married a Liverpool fan
I have a son who wants to be a Liverpool player
I have a son who wants to be a tree

And I stick their photos all
over my side of the bed,
and all down the skirting board,
they're all over our old
parana pine wardrobe
and even frescoes
on the window-sill,

just for when the
transfer market opens –
and I lose one of them.

Red

I am growing in this dress.

I plunge my wide curves
to the taut edges and
lift my shoulders to the
raspberry red,

I almost trust the seams.

Soft on my on my rounded stomach,
my breasts full,
my charcoal deep eyes.

I am growing into this dress,
it is wearing me, moving
me along the street,
clutching and gathering
in around my
rib-flesh holding me.

Soon I will be this dress.

Some evening
with laughter lines,
with less clutter in my head.

We will melt together.
But not this evening,
this evening is only practice,
this evening on
Grafton Street's cobbles,
this is only dress up.

Meon

for Caroline and Lorraine

Keep the meon
from our doors
and from our hearts,

lock our hearts up safe,

for meon bends her spine like
a cold little field mouse
and takes up nesting –

keep going,
keep spirit.

The stars sneak a
jealous look at us,
clattering up the cobbled
Quay Street stones
on a wet November night,
bright sequined handbags
tight under our oxters.

The stars don't look at our skirts
or our bright red lips,
but at our fight –

the way we throw
our heads back
laughing –

like we hadn't a care
in the world.

Boy

for Finn

I am made of sand silt and rock
I am boy of prayer
I am of war and hope and flotilla

Boy I am and I am made of my mother's fear

I am made from scratch and animal and grass and hail
I am boy of sound and light, of blood and bone and tusk
I am of forest and desert, of town and fruit

I am made of rum and berry and ebony

I am boy of name and sureness, of footfall and critic.

I am boy of rape

I am boy of fur, of pain, of shoe and igloo
I am boy of woman and wood, of car, train and truck
I am boy of love and lust
I am boy of sport and vein and blood
I am boy of deer and hunter and risk
I am boy of revolution
I am boy of protection
I am boy of upset
I am boy of joy
I am boy of nerve
I am boy of hair and rib
I am boy of Rory Gallagher
I am boy of Wham bars and open laces
I am boy of plastic
I am boy of no county
I am boy of church
I am boy of hugs and stage
I am boy of dolphin and whale

Boy I am and am I boy
of arrogance

I am boy of success
I am boy of tendon and courage
I am boy of tears and sobs
I am boy of a father's discontent
I am boy of ordinary
I am boy of bicycle and shape
I am boy of brother and protection
I am boy of envy and disillusion
I am boy of confusion
I am boy of stadium
I am boy of dance and song
I am boy of constellation and pyramid
I am boy of feud and oranges
I am boy of breast
I am boy of lust
I am boy of waves and froth
I am boy of surf and chest and sit-up
I am boy of attempt
I am boy of fail
I am boy of girl and kiss and midnight
I am boy of bench and wood and fire
I am boy of survival
I am boy of chance and flight and honour

I am boy of start point and stake boat
I am boy of journey's end
I am boy of saddle and handshake
I am boy of rust and rubric and red ink

I am cavalier
I am objector and difference
I am rebel and separatist

I am boy of anticipation
I am boy of gang and riot and coup

Boy I am, I am boy.

The People who Peopled me

wore overcoats
and turned
their capeens
backwards to
catch their honey sweat.

They wore aprons and kneaded
bread dough deep
from their shoulders.

The books they kept by
their place came only
from the *Reader's Digest*
or from God.

These people knew
God was good and
there was no word for sex.

Babies were the sun
and animals the bees
and neighbours were
the weather,
changeable but certain.

Monacle

My new lover told me never to
be intimidated,
square my shoulders,
sometimes that emperor is naked.

He told me at awkward times
when I mistake prose for
something doomfilled –
or I malaprop my way through
a convention on spectacular literature –
for spectacular literaturians,

drop my monacle to the
ground and fall to my hands
and my knees searching in
madness screaming,

oh my monacle!

Make new the focus love,
always make new the focus –

because they will die in the smoke
of the old guard burning.

And you will always have a monacle.

Birdsong

for Margaret

A gentle mother showers
her young daughters with
starlings, robins, oak trees,
dogs and cats and ash trees.

They play a game matching
the nests to the eggs
while shouting out;

Hell-London

Helen, your father's home from war again

The battle guns haven't
touched the sweet ditches
of the young Republic.

The gentle mother showers books
to her daughters' eager hands.

They train their ears to the birdsongs,
they keep house and routine,

the gentle woman is now old,

and she expects the absent daughters
to speak for her in return.

She recalls the Blue Tit of the Paridae family is loyal.

Then suddenly remembers that
dock leaves were used
as tea on family walks deep
in the woods.

She wonders where her own mother is.

The Erithacus Rubecula flies
winter warmth and they know his tune.

The young daughters, now old,
watch starlings nest in Raheny Ivy;

she notes they are chattery;
of the moment,
they make good company.

War

This is my son

This is

My Son

This. My. Son. Is.

My son is this

He is my son

This son, my is

This son

This is my son

My son

'Oxegen'

for Mark

When horses run,
they dig up soggy earth
with their dome hooves.

They fire it high to
the Leinster air
like moondancers
at a midsummer festival.

Mark fired me
over his shoulder
and splattered me
down on my back.

It was lashing the rain
away to the east,
over Punchestown –

A young pasty fella speaks,
chewing on his scabbed lip
sun-burned and soaked
sucking on a catheter
slung around his thigh –

God they always sound
like they knew it all
with that accent
the cunteens.

I hope it drowns them
over in England
the colonial fuckereens.

do ya want a suck?

G'wan

Don't tell me ye
like the fucking Brits?

We screamed at the naked rockers
sending us off to America.

A M E R I C A

As if anyone wanted to go there.

Skinny slips
of freckled parts.

The middle
Americans
on Omaha beach,

their first and last
passport –

delving terrified in the rain,

scores upon scores
of the poor bastards.

We had our battles brother –
We had had our Omaha –

Slithering along the wet soil,
pretending we had no story –

only honour.

Drowning

We are silent leaves from an oak
dropping in November's welcoming lap.

We are the silent swift legs of a rescue diver.

We are silent in morning's retaliation,
stewed coffee, angry children.

We are silent to the gift-horse
of the gutters,

the gripes of the tins and cans
that blow against
the pebble-dash.

We are silent to the dancers
and the dreams in our heads.

Silent to the sounds of nettle rile.
Silent to the treacherous rage of rhetoric.

In the dark we are
spontaneous with our bodies,
they battle the mimicry,

the raging blue iris,
the rough palms.

The misinterpretations of love.

After the age of Christ, I spoke.

Now peace is what
comes moments
after drowning.

Saucepans in the Sky

You point to the sky
and I cry laughing,

I'll never see it, I say —

Your Saucepans in the Sky.

The boys over in the Tavern
shoot pool,
watch Match of the Day
a mild March evening,

the gang at Largy drink
flagons of Buckkie
and cry for you
on this evening's bushing.

I lick your jaw
and taste
raspy bitter chocolate
from your cheap aftershave.

When you were dead,
just that minute,
the dead minute,

I could swear the sun came out.

I'm an angel
in a Monaghan ditch
waving my hands
from my sides
like a Spanish fan.

I'll find them;
wild constellations,
these saucepans in the sky.

One Direction

for Sinéad, Ciara and Órlaith

One has very floppy-hair.
One's from up the country,
the cutest.

One whose father
missed teaching him snooker
and bringing him down the pub.

The older girl is beautiful and intense
and stares at the cinema screen,
fleeting her almond eyes at the
boy beside her.

The younger is feisty and pretty and giggles,
she will fight for rights,
for freedom, for school trousers
and to go up town at lunch.

The older girl will mind her.

She'll take her by the hand
and with sure footfall,
soften her step
through the girl mines.

When the coast is clear,
and their life paths are paved,
they'll arch their long slender
spines and march on.

And the One Direction boys?

Oh they'll just be some boys
they used to know.

Man

I like plums, I say,
as you set the table.

You like plums too,
the stone isn't as annoying
as apple pips,
but far more lethal.

Your dark drooping eyes,
like the dog's eyes
before she died.

I hurried along the evening.
Rushing our lives to the routine drum.

I bath the children and sponge
their backs.
The small one, a miniature
of your narrow shoulders,
the same eyes transplanted
with a different hue
as if it sailed in a gentle
stream from the Barrow
to our bed.

We share a bottle of wine,
I watch you fall asleep.

The long retreat where your
dreams rattle you,
and you hunch up your shoulders,
protecting us from the door.

Just then, I think it was a man I captured.

Guilt

Why haven't you called or rang
or even just pulled your head
out from under the covers?

Stop staring at the bottom of the glass,
there'll be apple buds on the back of the blossoms

and you'll miss them girlie, you're too busy
gawking into that canal for a pram or two.

Staring in the slothy waters at the rusty iron with its
two fingered reflection.

Well you'll be sorry you've messed
this all up all over yourself again.

Because when you're all lonely in your hovel,
you'll need love.

There'll be crows picking the holes out of your eyes
and d'ya know what, you'll drive them to it.

You'll have no eyes, no eyes and it'll be your fault,
all that canal searching for rusty trolleys.

Mornings

All is calm again. Those few moments
of tearful destruction have thankfully
hidden. My child crouches like a rabbit
in the front porch waiting. Waiting for the calm
to come again on his mother's teary
face. They ask her where the rage comes from;
and she says amongst the flames and
the rotted crevices of her, where
coke slack and smog took home, where they lair
their fumes, and where the dead knights
dance the dance of the forgotten, and weep.
They ask her does it hurt, the rage and the
knights boldly dancing inside her like that,
like a torrent of fear? It only hurts
when they win, when the shields protects
their faces and their swords gut her heart.

ELAINE FEENEY teaches English at St. Jarlath's College, Tuam,
County Galway. She is considered part of a growing band of
new young political Irish poets. She won the North Beach
Nights Grand Slam and Cúirt Festival's Grand Slam. *The Radio
was Gospel* is Elaine's third collection, following *Indiscipline*
(2007) and *Where's Katie?* (Salmon, 2010). She has recorded an
audio collection of her work with Sarah Clancy, *Cinderella
Backwards* (2012). Her poetry has been broadcast on RTÉ radio
and television. Elaine was the Over The Edge poetry
competition judge in 2011 and NUI Galway's Sin poetry
competition judge in 2013. She has performed at various
literature and music festivals including the Cúirt International
Literature Festival, The Ex-Border Festival in Italy, The
Edinburgh Fringe Festival, The Vilenica Festival and The
Electric Picnic. Her work has been published in numerous
magazines including *The SHOp* and *The Stinging Fly*. Elaine's
work has been translated into Italian, Slovene and Lithuanian.
Elaine grew up in Athenry, Co. Galway, where she now lives
with her husband Ray Glasheen and sons, Jack and Finn.